# SCAFFOLDING THE LANGUAGE OF POWER

Scaffolding the Language of Power in Academia is a series of volumes that offers accessible, hands-on, scaffolded guides to developing the skills needed to successfully navigate writing across multiple milieus of academia.

The series works from the premise that doctoral level writing is part of the "language of power" in academia and has historically served as an exclusionary mechanism that keeps the doctorate largely white and male. However, it is also a genre that operates by particular rules, which can be taught in supportive and affirmative ways.

The series will include texts for multiple audiences, including textbooks and workbooks for 1) developing academic writing at the masters' and doctoral level, 2) supporting writing for peer-reviewed publications, and 3) building faculty pedagogical language knowledge and practice for supporting their students' writing development.

Volumes in the series include:

- Scaffolding the Language of Power: An Apprenticeship in Writing at the Doctoral Level (2024)
- Scaffolding the Language of Power: An Apprenticeship in Writing at the Doctoral Level Companion Workbook (2025)

The series editor, Dr. Kathryn (Katie) Strom, is a Professor of Educational Leadership and Director of the Center for Research on Equity and Collaborative Engagement at California State University, East Bay, as well as Hon. Associate Professor of Curriculum and Pedagogy at University College London. If you wish to have your proposal considered for inclusion in the series, please send a prospectus and your CV to Dr. Strom at kathryn.strom2@csueastbay.edu.

# SCAFFOLDING THE LANGUAGE OF POWER

An Apprenticeship in Writing
at the Doctoral Level

**COMPANION WORKBOOK**

**KATHRYN STROM**

Published by Myers Education Press, LLC
P.O. Box 424 Gorham, ME 04038



Myers Education Press is an academic publisher specializing in books, e-books, and digital content in the field of education. All of our books are subjected to a rigorous peer review process and produced in compliance with the standards of the Council on Library and Information Resources.

Library of Congress Cataloging-in-Publication Data available from Library of Congress.

13-digit ISBN 978-1-9755-0841-8 (paperback)

Printed in the United States of America.

All first editions printed on acid-free paper that meets the American National Standards Institute Z39-48 standard.

Books published by Myers Education Press may be purchased at special quantity discount rates for groups, workshops, training organizations, and classroom usage. Please call our customer service department at 1-800-232-0223 for details.

Editorial and graphic design by Kathryn Strom.

# How to Use This Workbook

This workbook is designed as a companion to *Scaffolding the Language of Power: An Apprenticeship in Doctoral Level Writing*. This workbook is most effective when used alongside the main textbook. Most of the exercises in the workbook build directly on concepts, frameworks, and examples presented in the corresponding chapters of *Scaffolding the Language of Power*. The workbook provides the expanded form of activities that appear in abbreviated form in the main text, as well as additional warm-ups, free-writes, guided writing exercises, and reflections. Each chapter contains warm-up activities that help you make personal connections to the concepts, guided practice exercises that scaffold your understanding of key writing moves, graphic organizers that deconstruct complex tasks, applications that help you generate text for your own dissertation, and metacognitive prompts to help you think about your own process.

**Here are three ways you can use this workbook:**

- ***As a Course Companion:*** If you're using Scaffolding the Language of Power in a doctoral writing course, this workbook provides ready-made activities for class discussions, individual assignments, and peer collaboration.
- ***As a Self-Guided Writing Tool:*** Doctoral students working independently can use this workbook to systematically develop their dissertation components. The activities build on each other to help you move from initial brainstorming to polished academic text.
- ***As a Targeted Resource:*** If you're struggling with specific aspects of doctoral writing—such as crafting arguments, synthesizing literature, or organizing complex ideas—you can focus on particular chapters that address your needs. However, make sure to review the foundational concepts in Chapters 1-3 before diving into specific sections.

Finally, I want to emphasize that there are many legitimate ways to approach doctoral-level writing. This workbook presents one particular approach—one that my EdD students have found helpful as they complete our fast-paced three-year doctoral program. But it is not *the way*. It is *a way*. As I discuss in the first chapter of the main text, there is no such thing as "the" way to write (or use language). Because we speak from where we are (or write from where we are, as the case may be), writing is not neutral nor one-size-fits-all. You bring a whole constellation of identities, experiences, beliefs, and intentions that will shape your writing. You can and should treat the ideas in this workbook as a minimum, and work with them, make them your own, to find a form of expression that feels authentic to you.

Happy writing!

# Table of Contents

# Section 1: A Three-Pronged Approach to Writing at the Doctoral Level

### 1. Warm-Up: 2-Part Reflection

**Part A.** Think back to your own educational experiences. Can you remember anyone (adults, peers, maybe even you yourself) referring to a "proper" or "correct" way to speak or write (e.g., "that's not proper English!")? What might they have meant by that—and what does using "proper" language look and sound like? Where does "proper" English come from, and who decided what was proper and what wasn't to begin with? Use the space below to free-write a reflection on the prompt above.

**Part B.** Now, read the introduction to chapter 1 and write a second reflection using these prompts: How did you expand your understanding from your original reflection? What questions do you have at this point about "academic" language?

**2. Different Perspectives on Language.** Compare and contrast the dominant western worldview with a critical perspective. What are some major differences between them? How is this applicable to language?

**3. Social Reproduction.** What is social reproduction—and how does it relate to language (and language at the doctoral level)? Can you think of any specific examples from your own experience?

**4. Culture of Power.** What is the culture of power and how does it relate to language? Can you think of any other examples of the culture of power?

**5. Systemic Functional Linguistics**. Describe systemic functional linguistics and the role of genre it in it. How do these ideas relate to doctoral literacy?

**6. Summarizing the Rules of the Language of Power.** Write a summary of your own understanding of the rules. Then, see if you can find an example of that characteristic, either in your own writing or in a peer-reviewed article you have read.

| | SUMMARY IN MY WORDS | EXAMPLE |
|---|---|---|
| Highly Organized and Scaffolded | | |
| Makes an Argument | | |
| Supported by Evidence | | |
| Detailed and Specific | | |
| Synthesis | | |
| Original Voice and Research | | |

**7. Self Assessment: The Rules of the Language of Power.** Use the table below to reflect on your strengths and areas of improvement.

| | What do I know already about this rule? What connected skills do I already have? | What do I want to learn about this rule? What connected skills do I need to learn? |
|---|---|---|
| Highly Organized and Scaffolded | | |
| Makes an Argument | | |
| Supported by Evidence | | |
| Detailed and Specific | | |
| Synthesis | | |
| Original Voice and Research | | |

**8. What is Scaffolding?** Open an internet browser and search for "Building Scaffolding." Choose a photo that shows the structure of scaffolding for a building. Click on the picture and describe the scaffolding you see, below. How would you describe the role of the scaffolding in the building process? What is it doing in the picture?

**9. Sociocultural Theory**. What is sociocultural theory? Summarize your understandings.

**10. Scaffolding and Learning.** What is scaffolding in the context of learning? Summarize your understandings.

**11. Chapter Reflection.** Write a reflection addressing the following questions:

- What are some of your take-aways from this section?
- Did you have any "aha's"?
- What connections can you make from what you learned to your own research and/or writing process?
- What questions are coming up for you at this point?

# Section 2. The Rules: Writing as a Pedagogical Act

1. **Warmup.** What is one type of writing you really excel at? (Personal narrative? Texting or emailing? Grant writing? Poetry? Songwriting? etc.) What is the purpose (or purposes) of that type of writing (what does it seek to do or achieve)? Now, imagine a really high-quality version of whatever type of writing you identified. What makes it high-quality? For example, what makes a really great poem, or email to parents, or grant narrative? Add your thoughts below.

| TYPE OF WRITING | PURPOSE(S) | QUALITY CHARACTERISTICS |
|---|---|---|
| | | |

2. **Writing Purpose and Quality.** Examine what you wrote, above. How do those quality markers you just identified relate to the purpose? How does the writer use those quality characteristics to help meet the goals of that type of writing?

**3. Purposes of Doctoral Level Writing.** Now, make connections to doctoral level literacy. What do you think are some of the purposes of language at the doctoral level? What are some of the characteristics of high-quality writing at the doctoral level? How do those characteristics help meet the purposes you named?

**4. Scaffolding and Writing**. What does it mean to ***scaffold*** as a writing strategy? What are your thoughts about this pedagogical approach to writing?

**5. Scaffolding Strategies**. Consider the strategies below. Which ones are you familiar with? How do you think they might support the reader?

| SCAFFOLDING STRATEGY | LEVEL OF FAMILIARITY | HOW I THINK IT SUPPORTS THE READER |
|---|---|---|
| **Chunking and Headings** | | |
| **Road Maps** | | |
| **Topic Sentences** | | |
| **Connectors and Transitions** | | |
| **Signal Words and Phrases** | | |

**6. Chunking**. What is chunking? How does it help the reader?

**7. Headings.** How do headings support the reader? What are the things to keep in mind when creating headings?

**8. Practicing Chunking and Headings.** Below, use brackets to chunk each section. Write headings out to the left where you think each section would start.

| | |
|---|---|
| | Complexity theories refer to a set of explanatory frameworks that focus on the spontaneous emergence of phenomena out of what might seem to be chaos. As there is not one agreed-upon complexity perspective, the summary we provide is consistent with conceptual and empirical work utilizing complexity science in the field of social science research (e.g., Byrne, 1998; Clarke & Collins, 2007; Davis & Sumara, 1997/2006; Mason, 2008). According to this interpretation, human activity (such as teaching/learning), occurs at the edge of chaos (Butz, 1997; Waldrop, 1992) which introduces conditions to which the system must collectively adapt and grow.<br>Existing in at "the edge of chaos" means that a system exists in a state with enough disequilibrium to spur growth, but not enough to plunge it into total disorder (Waldrop, 1992). The edge of chaos concept is analogous to Piaget's (1954) notion of cognitive dissonance—that is, a certain amount of conflict must must occur for us to learn. Likewise, the presence of some disequilibrium is vital for systems to be considered "living," because it spurs systems to shift and adapt to better allow for survival in always-changing circumstances (Clarke & Collins, 2007). In the case of beginning teachers, much of their first-year teaching is characterized by major dissonance of one kind or another, not the least of which often entails a misalignment between the ideals espoused by their teacher preparation programs and the realities of schools (Cook, 2009; Veenman, 1984). However, for new teachers to continue to learn and grow on the edge of chaos and ultimately survive their first year of teaching, the disequilibrium they experience must not be too severe. To ensure personal survival under these conditions, the teacher may change schools or leave the profession entirely.<br>Systems interacting on the edge of chaos are nested—that is, they are simultaneously an autonomous system, a system of systems, and embedded in a larger system (Davis & Sumara, 1997, 2006). Because of their nestedness—both arising from and being part of other complex systems while being a system in and of itself— their boundaries tend to be fluid and overlapping (Davis & Sumara, 2006). As we discuss in the findings section, nested within beginning teaching are: the first-year teacher system (the micro-level, including the teacher's preservice learning; her beliefs about self, students, teaching, and learning; and her personal qualities, background, and needs); the classroom system (the meso level, including the teacher, the students, available resources, and the physical environment); the school system (the macro level, including the administrators, teachers, mentors, parents, school culture, school structures, the level of difficulty of the novice's teaching assignment, and accessibility of professional support resulting from school-university partnerships); and larger educational systems (the super-macro level, including the district and broader policy landscape). |

**9. Road Maps.** What are road maps? How do they support the reader?

**10. Road Map Practice.** If you came across the following road map at the beginning of a section of a paper, what hints does it give you about the big ideas that will be covered in the paragraphs that follow?

*Non-human elements in the school system, including the collective school culture, school structures, and school-university partnerships, can also shape first-year teacher practices by serving as constraining and/or enabling forces. (Strom et al., 2018, p. 23)*

**11. Topic Sentences.** What are topic sentences? How do they support the reader?

**12. Topic Sentence Analysis.** What is the topic sentence in the paragraph below (Strom & Viesca, 2021, p. 220)? Highlight or underline it. How does it help the reader understand the main idea of the paragraph?

*One of the most important ontological shifts involved in this proposed complex framework of learning-practice involves a move from being to becoming, along with an understanding that the process of becoming is one of continual differentiation (Deleuze and Guattari 1987, Braidotti 2013). This move entails disrupting a view of the world as ordered and static and instead acknowledging that reality is dynamic and alive, always changing, a view of reality that Braidotti (2006) has termed 'process ontology'. Not only is the world always in process, always becoming, but more precisely, the process is one of relationality– a 'becoming-with', or as Haraway (2016) proposes, a making with. Further, becomings are always multiple – since activity occurs with/in assemblages, these transformations occur in relation to other elements, both human and non-human. When a process ontology is adopted, then, questions of 'what' become much less important (since the 'what' changes from moment to moment). Instead, questions of 'how', of relations that enable becomings, become vital (Strom and Martin, 2017).*

**13. Topic Sentence Relationality.** Underline the topic sentence in the following paragraph (from Strom & Martin, 2022, p. 3). How does each sentence that follows it relate to it (unpacking the ideas, expanding, illustrating, etc.)?

*Another key critical posthuman concept is distributive agency (Bennett, 2009), a key characteristic of assemblages. This concept suggests people are not autonomous, self-regulating, conscious actors, but instead share agency with all elements of an assemblage, both human and non. Distributive agency decenters the human actor or participant in the assemblage and foregrounds relationality, as well as highlights the role and influence of the non-human (Strom & Viesca, 2021) and the vitality of matter itself (Bennett, 2009). In teaching, distributive agency presents an important counter-argument to the taken-for-granted notion that teaching is a one-way transaction that teachers "do" to students. Instead, teaching is a collective activity that is jointly produced by the collaborative activity of teacher-students-space-content-context plus (Strom, 2015).*

**14. Topic Sentence Application.** Choose a paragraph from your own work to analyze. Write the topic sentence in the space below. Then, describe how each of the following sentences relates to it.

**15. Basic Transitions.** Read the following paragraph. What are the purposes of the highlighted transitions? How do you know?

| EXCERPT | TRANSITION PURPOSE |
|---|---|
| **Therefore,** the development of teacher subjectivity and teaching practice is not a linear process: **that is**, it is not the end result of completing a teacher preparation program, attaining state licensure, and gaining employment in a school. **Instead,** becoming a teacher is an intra-active process: teacher preparation programs, schools, and policy assemblages work together to produce teacher subjectivity. **For example,** the intra-actions within a kindergarten classroom with the students, the material resources (tables, toys, crayons, paints, scissors), the time (weekdays between the hours of 8:00 a.m.-3:00 p.m.), the discourse (ideas relevant to the content areas of mathematics, literacy, and so on), and spatial engagement (the adult moves about the room as the students work at their tables) intra-act to enable the recognition of the adult in this space and time as "teacher"). (Strom & Martin, 2022, p. 3) | |

**16. Basic Transition Practice.** Find a paper and identify a paragraph to work with. Analyze your use of basic transitions in the paragraph. What purpose does each serve? How does it help with the flow of ideas?

**17. Strategic Repetition.** What is "strategic repetition" as a writing pattern? How does strategic repetition help with idea flow? How do you think it helps support your reader?

**18. Synonyms.** How is using synonyms a connector strategy? How does it support your reader?

**19. Pronouns.** How is using pronouns a connector strategy? How does it support the reader?

**20. Connector (Referent) Phrases.** What are connector (or referent) words and phrases? How do they support the reader?

**21. Transition and Connector Practice.** Analyze the following paragraph. Identify the basic transitions, strategic repetition, synonyms, pronouns, and connector words/referent phrases that help build a logical flow from the first sentence to the last. How do these help support the reader to follow my line of thinking?

*Assemblage, in particular, helps shift away from a view of the world as populated by agentic individuals and toward one consisting of multiplicities with distributed agency. An assemblage is a mixture of humans, things, ideas, and conditions that interact and produce something (Strom, 2015). For example, a classroom is an assemblage, consisting of the teacher, students, the physical space, desks, academic content, contextual conditions, and so on (deFreitas, 2012). An assemblage is not just a particular grouping, but also refers to the way those work together to produce knowledge, action, or other happenings in particular ways. Thus, assemblage is an analytic tool to help us analyze the situated, multi-faceted, interactional activity of teaching.*

**22. Transition and Connector Application.** Pick a paragraph from a paper you have written. In the lefthand column, write each sentence of the paragraph, in order. In the righthand column, analyze your use of transitions and connectors. Ask yourself the following: What basic transitions are you using and why? What are they connecting and signaling? How are you using pronouns? Are the referents clear? What connectors or referent phrases are you using? What words or phrases are you using for strategic repetition? What synonyms are you using?

| SENTENCE | TRANSITION/CONNECTOR ANALYSIS |
| --- | --- |
| | |
| | |
| | |
| | |
| | |
| | |

**23. Signal Words and Phrases.** What are signal words and phrases? How do they support the reader?

**24. Signaling Analysis.** How is signaling used to help organize the paragraph below and provide scaffolding for the reader? Identify the signaling words/phrases then analyze how they support the reader, using the chart below.

*Sociocultural theory (Vygotsky, 1978) has five main principles. First, learning is social and occurs through interaction. Second, it is mediated by tools or artifacts such as language, which is why dialogue is so important in the learning process. Third, learning happens first inter-personally, as students talk, and then intra-personally, as they internalize their learning. Fourth, learning occurs in the "zone of proximal development," or the area just beyond what students are capable of doing by themselves, as they receive tailored assistance or "scaffolding" to stretch themselves to grasp the knowledge or skill. Finally, learning can be observed as changes in participation.*

| SIGNAL WORD OR PHRASE | HOW IT SUPPORTS THE READER |
|---|---|
| | |
| | |
| | |
| | |
| | |

**25. Chapter Reflection.** Write a reflection addressing the following questions:

- What are some of your take-aways about organization and scaffolding?
- Did you have any "aha's" from this section?
- What scaffolding strategies do you think will be most effective for your own writing? Why?
- What questions are coming up for you at this point?

# Section 3. The Rest of the Rules of the Language of Power

**1. Warm-Up.** Read through the "rules" again in chapter 2 of *Scaffolding the Language of Power.* Which do you think is your strongest point? Which do you think you need the most practice with? Explain.

**2. Making a Well-Reasoned Argument.** What is your understanding of an *argument?* What does a high-quality argument look like?

**3. Analyzing Your Work.** Choose an argument you've made in one of your doctoral papers. Brainstorm out the pieces below.

| | |
|---|---|
| **Claim** | |
| **Explanation** | |
| **Support** | |

**4. Analyzing an Argument.** Read the following paragraph from Strom et al. (2018, p. 3). What is the claim the author is making in this excerpt? What reasoning is provided to persuade the reader that this claim is plausible or believable?

*In the case of first-year teaching, complexity theory— the study of complex, living systems— helps conceptualize novice practices as arising from interactions occurring between the teacher and other elements within a larger network. As such, complexity theory enables an examination of the forces that coalesce on multiple planes to produce first-year teaching practices. This perspective provides an ecological approach to conceptualizing teaching practice that examines phenomena as a whole, rather than merely focusing on their parts (Cochran-Smith, et al., 2014).*

**5. Analyzing an Argument.** Read the following excerpt from Strom and Martin (2023, p. 4). Identify the two claims the author makes in this excerpt. What reasoning is provided to persuade the reader that this claim is plausible or believable?

*Teacher practice is also mediated by their beliefs about teaching and learning (e.g., Bergeron, 2008; Starkey, 2010). As an example, in the New Zealand context, Starkey (2010) examined first-year teachers' use of technology and found that their traditional beliefs regarding mathematics learning (i.e., that working out problems with paper and pencil was most effective) interfered with their ability to integrate technology into their lessons. Teachers' backgrounds and experiences also have the potential to impact teaching (e.g., Birrell, 1995; Coffey & Farinde-Wu, 2016; Newman, 2010). Newman (2010), for instance, interviewed beginning teachers in the U.K. who entered the profession after a career change and reported that their previous career experiences influenced the way they approached pedagogy.*

**6. Supporting Arguments with Evidence.** Write a reflection on the following: What is your understanding of evidence? Why is it important in your dissertation? What might be some of the different types of evidence you would draw on to support your arguments or claims?

**7. Finding Evidence.** Make a list of the top 10 peer-reviewed journals that will be relevant for your topic.

| | JOURNAL NAME |
|---|---|
| 1 | |
| 2 | |
| 3 | |
| 4 | |
| 5 | |
| 6 | |
| 7 | |
| 8 | |
| 9 | |
| 10 | |

**8. Identifying Kinds of Research Texts.** Find examples of empirical, conceptual, and lit review articles. What language and text features does each have?

| ARTICLE TYPE | CITATIONS | LANGUAGE & TEXT FEATURES |
|---|---|---|
| Empirical Examples | | |
| Conceptual Examples | | |
| Literature Review Examples | | |

**9. Professional Organizations.** Make a list of professional organizations or entties in your field or that are relevant to your topic. Look up their websites to see if they might have reports or data that might be useful to you.

| ORGANIZATION NAME | DESCRIPTION | WEBSITE |
| --- | --- | --- |
| | | |
| | | |
| | | |
| | | |

**10. Top Scholars in your Field**. Make a list of the top scholars in your field. Using your school library website or Google scholar, search to see if they have books that may be relevant to your topic.

| SCHOLAR NAME | ARTICLES AND BOOKS OF INTEREST |
| --- | --- |
| | |
| | |
| | |
| | |
| | |
| | |

**11. Detailed, Specific, Precise Language.** Reflect on the three language features below. How would you define the word generally? What do you think it would look like in doctoral writing (e.g., what does it mean to be detailed in your dissertation writing)?

| FEATURE | GENERAL DEFINITION | WHAT IT LOOKS LIKE IN DOCTORAL WRITING |
|---|---|---|
| Detailed | | |
| Specific | | |
| Precise | | |

**12. Detail, Specificity, and Precision in Problem Statements.** Read the two examples below of a brief problem statement. What differences do you see between the two? How do these a) increase the level of detail, specificity, and/or precision and b) support the reader in understanding the problem driving the study?

- **Sentence 1:** *New teachers often abandon their preservice learning and adopt traditional practices.*
- **Sentence 2:** *New teachers often abandon the student-centered and equity-minded practices learned in their preservice programs and adopt instead transmission-oriented, technicist teaching practices.*

**13. Detail, Specificity, and Precision in Purpose Statements.** Read the two examples below of a study purpose statement. What differences do you see between the two? What new information is added in the second sentence? How do those improvements a) increase the level of detail, specificity, and/or precision; and b) support the reader in better understanding the study and what it will investigate?

- **Sentence 1:** *This study examines the ways that three new teachers negotiated their preservice learning in their new settings.*
- **Sentence 2:** *This qualitative multiple case study examines the ways that three first-year high school science teachers negotiated their preservice learning with human and contextual elements in their new classroom settings.*

**14. Detail, Specificity, and Precision in Theoretical Frameworks.** Read the two examples below of a sentence from a theoretical framework. What differences do you see between the two? What new information is added in the second sentence? How do those improvements a) increase the level of detail, specificity, and/or precision and b) support the reader in better understanding teaching as a co-constructed phenomenon?

- **Sentence 1:** *Teaching arises from joint activity of multiple human actors and nonhuman elements.*
- **Sentence 2:** *From a rhizomatic perspective, teaching arises from joint activity of multiple human actors (e.g., teachers, students, colleagues, administrators) and nonhuman elements (e.g., content, physical space, school cultures, bell schedules).*

**15. Application to Your Own Work.** Choose an assignment you have completed from a doctoral class. Use the following activities to reflect on and assess your writing in terms of details and specificity.

| Identify an example from your work where you use specific, precise language. | In what ways is the language specific and precise? How does this support your reader's understanding? |
| --- | --- |
| | |

| Identify an example from your work where you use provide a high level of detail. | Explain the details that are included. How do they support your reader's understanding? |
| --- | --- |
| | |

| **Identify an example where you use vague language.** | **What words or phrases could you add to increase the level of detail and specificity?** |
|---|---|
| | |

| **Identify an example where you could use more detail.** | **If you were someone without background knowledge on this topic, would you be able to access all the ideas? List terms or ideas that might need brief definitions, examples, context, or other elaboration.** |
|---|---|
| | |

| Now, use those words/phrases to revise your original writing in the examples you identified above. |
|---|
| |

**16. Striving for Synthesis over Summary.** Define summary and synthesis. What are the characteristics or features of each?

| | DEFINITION AND CHARACTERISTICS |
|---|---|
| Summary | |
| Synthesis | |

**17. Distinguishing Synthesis.** Read the excerpt below (Strom, Margolis, & Polat, 2019, p. 2) on teacher dispositions. Is it a summary or a synthesis? What are features or characteristics of the writing that tell you? What do you think the purpose of this synthesis is?

*One tension evident in various definitions of teacher dispositions is the extent to which they reside either in the attributes or the actions of the individual teacher. For example, NCATE (2001) defines dispositions as the former: "The values, commitments, and professional ethics that influence behaviors towards students, families, colleagues, and communities and affect student learning, motivation, development, as well as the educator's own professional growth. Dispositions are guided by beliefs and attitudes related to values such as caring, fairness, honesty, responsibility, and social justice"(NCATE, 2001, p. 30). Language like "values," "beliefs," and "attitudes" locates dispositions primarily within the psyche of the teacher while phrases like "are guided by" imply causal relationships with other cognitive traits, an approach that only diminishes the possibility of a sound operational definition of the term. Similarly, Damon (2007) defines dispositions as "... a trait or characteristic that is embedded in temperament and disposes a person toward certain choices" (p. 376). The linking of the word "trait" with "dispose" places dispositions somewhere within the teacher's internal world. On the other hand, others have promoted a more action-centered definition of teacher dispositions. For example, Villegas (2007) argues that dispositions are "tendencies" for particular behaviors, but they are made concrete in the behavior itself.*

**18. A Deeper Look at Synthesis.** Take a look at the example below. How is the author synthesizing literature to paint a broader picture? What do you think her purpose is?

*It is little wonder that many believe educational leadership itself is in a crisis. Some relate the crisis to a lack of qualified candidates for superintendencies (Esparo & Rader, 2001) or school principalships (Chirichello, 2001; Malone & Caddell, 2000). Others believe that the crisis has occurred as a result of naïve, conservative, and traditional leadership responses to increasingly complex, challenging, and postmodern educational contexts (Maxcy, 1994). Giroux (1992) associates difficulties of educational leadership with crises of democratic government. Still others are concerned about the lack of leadership offered by school boards themselves (van Alfen, 1993) or about the propensity of educators to adopt a series of reforms in rapid succession (Fullan, 2003), failing to empower either teachers or administrators. (Shields, 2010, p. 110)*

**19. Synthesis Guided Practice.** Summarize the key ideas from each of the definitions of "qualitative research" in your own words.

| Definition | Summary |
| --- | --- |
| Qualitative research is generally characterized by inductive approaches to knowledge building aimed at generating meaning. Researchers use this approach to explore; to robustly investigate and learn about social phenomenon; to unpack the meanings people ascribe to activities, situations, events, or artifacts; or to build a depth of understanding about some dimension of social life. The values underlying qualitative research include the importance of people's subjective experiences and meaning-making processes and acquiring a depth of understanding (i.e., detailed information from a small sample). Qualitative research is generally appropriate when your primary purpose is to explore, describe, or explain. (Leavy, 2017, p. 9) | **Your summary of key ideas:** |
| Qualitative research ... consists of a set of interpretive, material practices that make the world visible. These practices transform the world. They turn the world into a series of representations, including field notes, interviews, conversations, photographs, recordings, and memos to the self. At this level, qualitative research involves an interpretive, naturalistic approach to the world. This means that qualitative researchers study things in their natural settings, attempting to make sense of, or interpret, phenomena in terms of the meanings people bring to them. (Denzin & Lincoln, 2005, p. 3) | **Your summary of key ideas:** |
| Qualitative researchers are interested in understanding ... how people make sense of their world and the experiences they have in the world ... The following four characteristics are identified by most as key to understanding the nature of qualitative research: the focus is on process, understanding, and meaning; the researcher is the primary instrument of data collection and analysis; the process is inductive; and the product is richly descriptive. (Merriam, 2009, p. 13-14) | **Your summary of key ideas:** |
| [In qualitative research] the information or data collected and analyzed is primarily ... nonquantitative in character, consisting of textual materials such as interview transcripts, fieldnotes, and documents, and/or visual materials such as artifacts, photographs, video recordings, and Internet sites, that document human experiences about others and/or one's self in social action and reflexive states. ... Outcomes are most often composed of essential representations and presentations of salient findings from the analytic synthesis of data and can include: documentation of cultural observations, new insights and understandings about individual and social complexity, evaluation of the effectiveness of programs or policies, artistic renderings of human meanings, and/or the critique of existing social orders and the initiation of social justice. (Saldaña, 2011, p. 3) | **Your summary of key ideas:** |

| **Part 2. Use your notes from the exercise above to create a single definition of 1-3 sentences that integrates information from across the four sources. Use your own words.** |
|---|
| |

**19. Synthesis Application.** Choose one concept or big idea that is (or you think will be) central to your research (e.g., *identity, feminism, culturally relevant instruction,* etc*).* Find at least three different excerpts from different sources that offer definitions and/or descriptions of the concept/idea. List the source on one side and summarize the main ideas on the other. Then, synthesize the key ideas into a one- to two-sentence definition.

| **CONCEPT/IDEA** | |
|---|---|
| **AUTHOR(S), YEAR** | **KEY IDEAS (IN YOUR OWN WORDS)** |
| | |
| | |
| | |
| | |

| Synthesize these notes into a single definition, in your own words, of 1-2 sentences that integrates information from all sources. |
| --- |
| |

**20. Using Quotes with Purpose.** Identify three recent articles and skim them for quote usage. Choose several quotes and analyze them for purpose using the graphic organizer below. Use the organizer below to analyze them for purpose.

| PURPOSE | QUOTE | HOW DOES IT ACHIEVE ITS PURPOSE? |
| --- | --- | --- |
| Emphasize a point | | |
| Illustrate a point | | |
| Provide evidence for a point | | |
| Convey original aesthetics, power, or poignance | | |

**21. Quote Analysis.** Read the following excerpt from Zeichner (2010, p. 1546).

*The solution to the teacher quality problem according to some is to deregulate teacher education and open the gates to individuals who have not completed a teacher education program prior to certification (e.g., Hess, 2009; Walsh, 2004) rather than to improve the conditions in public schools that are driving teachers out. Andrew Rosen, president of Kaplan College, which is part of one of the major for-profit teacher education companies to enter the U.S. teacher education market in recent years stated the following in an online conversation about teacher education that clearly illustrates this stance: "Teaching is less lucrative and is rife with work environment issues that many deem not to be worthy of investment. By reducing the barriers for bright-minded professionals, we can increase the population of qualified candidates" (Rosen, 2003).*

| | |
|---|---|
| **What is his purpose in using this quote?** | |
| **How does he introduce the quote?** | |
| **What language does he use to let the reader know why quote is being used?** | |

**22. Quote Analysis: Further Practice.** Read the quote below from Strom (2014, p. 59). This quote appears in the literature review section of the dissertation.

*Brashier and Norris (2008), investigating the practices of 25 early grade teachers to identify factors that affected teachers' use of certain developmentally appropriate strategies, found that several study participants reduced—but did not necessarily abandon—their use of such practices to quell conflict in their classrooms. One teacher discussed the tension between ensuring orderly conduct and maintaining developmentally appropriate practice as follows: "I feel like this time of the day is the most fun and one of the most meaningful (as far as learning goes) parts of the day for my students, but more children get in trouble during this time too. I see tendencies to become too loud, and even too violent. My students don't hit or push much, but in centers and at recess, it tends to happen a lot" (p. 35).*

| | |
|---|---|
| **What is the purpose of the quote in this passage?** | |
| **How does the author contextualize, or explain, the quote?** | |
| **How does the quote support the main point of the passage?** | |

**23. Quote Application.** Select a paper you wrote for one of your past doctoral classes and find a passage from that contains a direct quote.

| | |
|---|---|
| **Copy and paste the passage with the quote here.** | |
| **Critique your use of the quote. What is the purpose of the quote in that passage, and is the purpose of the quote clear to your reader? Is it introduced and explained?** | |
| **If you answered "no" to any of the questions above, edit the passage and paste the new version here.** | |
| **Explain what edits you made and why.** | |

**24. Chapter Reflection.** Write a reflection addressing the following questions:

- What are some of your take-aways from this section?
- Did you have any "aha's" about the rest of the framework?
- Which of the "rules" of this chapter do you think you have a good handle on, and which do you think you will need to work harder to learn?
- What questions are coming up for you at this point?

# Section 4. The Problem Statement

**1. 3-Part Warm-up.**

**A.** What do you want to study, and why?

**B.** What is the underlying problem or issue that your study responds to?

**C.** Why is it a problem, and how do you know?

**2. Purposes of the Problem Statement.** In the organizer below, summarize your understanding of the major goals of the problem statement and sketch out some initial thoughts on what that element might look like for you.

| | |
|---|---|
| **Clearly Describe the Problem** | |
| **Sketch the Problem Background** | |
| **Provide a Compelling Rationale** | |
| **Define Key Concepts** | |
| **Provide an Overview of the Study** | |

**3. Citation Charts.** As you read, keep a chart of citations with notes on the relevance of the reading to the problem you are articulating (suggested format below).

| | |
|---|---|
| **Citation** | |
| **What is the problem?** | |
| **Where does the problem come from?**<br>**Why does it persist?** | |
| **What evidence shows the significance and urgency of the problem?** | |
| **Quotes and notes** | |

**4. Reflective Memo.** Every 3-5 texts you read, stop and write a reflective memo. Use the space below to practice writing one, exploring the following prompts in light of your reading: 1) What is the problem? 2) Where did the problem come from, or why does it persist? 3)How do I know it is a problem (what evidence is there)?

**5. Name the Problem.** Building on the thinking from the warm-up in the beginning of the chapter, articulate what you want to study and the problem that study would respond to.

| | |
|---|---|
| **Study Focus/ Purpose:** What do you want to examine or investigate, and what do you hope to accomplish as a result? | |
| **Study Problem:** What is the issue driving the study—the thing you hope to change, improve, or address in some way? | |

**6. Problem Text Generation.** Using the text you developed for the study problem, brainstorm at least 3 different ways to write it in a single complete sentence.

| | |
|---|---|
| 1 | |
| 2 | |
| 3 | |

**7. Set the Context.** To begin your problem summary paragraph, you need to set the stage a little with some context. What kind of background information or other contextual details might help you introduce the problem? Free-write below.

| |
|---|
| |

**8. Strategies for Presenting Information.** Three key strategies for presenting information in the problem summary include using a powerful quote, illustrating with statistics, or beginning with a story or scenario that helps bridge into the problem. Try out the strategies below.

| | |
|---|---|
| **Powerful Quote** | |
| **Statistics** | |
| **Story or Scenario** | |

**9. Provide Details.** Use the organizer below to generate ideas on each of the dimensions of the problem summary.

| | |
|---|---|
| **What:** Define *what* the problem is. | |
| **Who:** Describe *who* the problem affects. | |
| **Why:** Describe *why* it is a problem. | |
| **How:** Describe *how* we know it is a problem. | |

**10. Support with Evidence.** Building on the "how" row above, locate several pieces of evidence that illustrate the problem, its impact, or anything related. Summarize each piece of evidence in your own words with a citation. Then, reflect on how this evidence supports your reasoning about the problem, and how you might use it to build a persuasive argument.

| **Evidence** (Your summary + short citation) | **Reflection:** In what way does this evidence support claims about the problem? How might you use this evidence in your problem summary paragraph? |
|---|---|
| | |
| | |
| | |
| | |
| | |

**11. Locating the Entrypoint.** Most studies will further narrow the problem, identifying a particular dimension or entry point within the larger issue. Use the organizer below to generate text.

| | |
|---|---|
| **Need:** What areas of the problem are most urgent to address? What areas need more study? | |
| **Interest:** What particular areas of the problem are you most interested in? | |
| **Access:** What areas of the problem are you most well-positioned to research? | |
| **Feasibility:** What areas or topics within the larger problem would you be able to practically research in the time you have? | |

**12. Drafting the Problem Summary.** Use the text you have generated in the previous activities to draft out sentences that you can edit into the problem summary section.

| SUMMARY ELEMENT | DRAFT SENTENCE(S) | EVIDENCE |
|---|---|---|
| Write 1-2 sentences that set the context for the problem. | | |
| Write 1 sentence that clearly states the problem. | | |
| Write 1-3 sentences that provide additional details about the problem. | | |
| Write 1-2 sentences that narrow the problem | | |

**13. Exploring the Problem Background.** Off the top of your head, what pieces of information does your reader need to understand the problem driving your study, where that problem came from, and why it persists? Challenge yourself to write at least three ideas down.

**14. Background vs. Literature Review.** What are some of the key differences of the problem background and the literature review? What questions do you still have?

**15. Background Information Idea Generation.** Use the questions below to jot down important topics or ideas to include in your problem background section. Some of these may overlap.

| | |
|---|---|
| **Roots:** Where did the problem come from? What created it? | |
| **Current Context:** What is happening in education right now that is making the problem especially urgent to solve? | |
| **Policies, Programs, or Concepts:** Are there any important policies, programs, or concepts that need to be discussed? | |
| **Foreshadowed Information:** What information did you introduce in the problem summary that you need to explain in more detail? | |

**16. Problem Dimensions.** As an alternative, consider these common problem dimensions. Bullet out your thoughts for each. Can you think of other dimensions? Add them to the bottom rows that have been left blank for you.

| | |
|---|---|
| **Historical Dimension** | |
| **Political Dimension** | |
| **Sociocultural Dimension** | |
| **Institutional or Organizational Dimension** | |
| | |
| | |

**17. Background Memo.** Use your thinking from the activities above and free write using the following prompt: What 3-4 main topics do you think would be most important for your reader to know about the problem to understand its origins, development, and/or persistence? Describe each problem briefly and provide a rationale.

**18. Outlining the Background.** Use the three organizers below to outline your background statement. Think through the factor, your main assertion, other details to include, and supporting evidence. Finally, reflect on what you've written and how it will help the reader understand the problem better.

| **BACKGROUND OR CONTRIBUTING FACTOR 1** | |
|---|---|
| **Main Assertion** | |
| **Other Claims and Details** | |
| **Evidence to Support Claims** | |
| **Reflection:** How does this factor help us understand the problem? | |

| **BACKGROUND OR CONTRIBUTING FACTOR 2** | |
|---|---|
| **Main Assertion** | |
| **Other Claims and Details** | |
| **Evidence to Support Claims** | |
| **Reflection:** How does this factor help us understand the problem? | |

| **BACKGROUND OR CONTRIBUTING FACTOR 3** | |
|---|---|
| **Main Assertion** | |
| **Other Claims and Details** | |
| **Evidence to Support Claims** | |
| **Reflection:** How does this factor help us understand the problem? | |

**19. Exploring the Problem Rationale.** Free-write: Why does this issue need to be urgently addressed? How do you know? What specifically do we need to research to be able to address it? How do you know we need to do that?

**20. Building Out the Practical Rationale.** In the table below, use your reading notes to bullet out information you have on short/long-term impacts and how those relate to larger society issues. Then, from those bullets, draft impact statements to work with and add your supporting evidence for them.

| | BULLETED NOTES | IMPACT CLAIM(S) | EVIDENCE |
|---|---|---|---|
| **Short Term Impacts** | | | |
| **Long term Impacts** | | | |
| **Connection to Larger Societal Issues** | | | |

**21. Draft of Practical Rationale.** Sketch out 1-2 paragraphs, using the text you generated in the activity above. Be sure to use a topic sentence and transition/connector words.

**22. Building out the Research Rationale.** Jot down notes answering each question to the best of your availability. Come back and revise it once you've completed your lit review and formally articulated the gap.

| | |
|---|---|
| **What do we know about the issue from research?** | |
| **What do we NOT know (the gap in research)?** | |
| **How will your project address this gap?** | |

**23. Exploring the Purpose Statement.** Describe what you would like to do in your study in practical terms. What are your goals—what do you hope it will achieve or do?

| |
|---|
| |

**24. Build Out Your Purpose Sentence.** Use the organizer below, which lists each of the elements of a purpose statement, to generate text for your purpose sentence.

| | ELEMENTS OF THE PURPOSE SENTENCE |
|---|---|
| Signal Phrase | |
| Purpose Verb | |
| Method/ Methodology | |
| Phenomenon/a | |
| Participants and Setting | |

**25. Purpose Sentence Draft.** Use the elements above to craft a draft purpose sentence.

**26. Align Research Purpose and Questions.** In the organizer below, add your purpose and draft research questions. Then, edit the research question(s) so that it is clear to your reader how they will meet the purpose.

| | |
|---|---|
| **Research Purpose** | |
| **Research Questions** | |

**27. Build Out Your Contributions Statement.** In the organizer below, generate thinking regarding what your study's concrete, short term outcomes will be, and what you hope the broader impact could be. For each, articulate how this outcome connects back to the problem framing your study. Then, identify the language you used to make those connections.

| | |
|---|---|
| **Short-Term Outcome (Concrete)** | |
| **Broader impact (Speculative)** | |
| **Language Used** | |

**28. Contribution Sentence Draft.** Use the elements from the previous organizer to craft your contribution sentence.

**29. Putting it all together.** Use the elements from the last several activities to craft your purpose paragraph.

**29. Optional Activity:** Reverse outline the logic of the entire problem statement. Summarize each of the elements below, then examine the overall logic.

| | |
|---|---|
| **Problem** | |
| **Factors that Explain the Problem** | |
| **Practical Rrationale** | |
| **Research Rationale** | |
| **Purpose** | |
| **Questions** | |
| **Contributions** | |

**30. Chapter Reflection.** Write a reflection addressing the following questions:

- What are some of your take-aways from this chapter about crafting a compelling problem statement?
- Did you have any "aha's" about writing your own problem and/or purpose statement?
- What questions are coming up for you at this point about articulating your research problem, connecting it to background factors, or developing your purpose statement?

# Section 5. The Literature Review

**1. Activating Previous Knowledge about Literature Reviews.** Take 3-5 minutes and jot down ideas that come to your mind about the following questions:

- What do you know about empirical literature reviews?
- What questions or wonderings do you have about empirical literature reviews?
- What kinds of topics do you think you will need to read about?

**2. Examining Literature Review Structure.** Find a dissertation on your topic and download it. Locate the literature review (typically this is found in chapter two). Skim the literature review using the following prompts.

| | | |
|---|---|---|
| **Find the literature review introduction.** | ***What information is offered there?*** | |
| | ***Does the author provide a clear roadmap of their lit review structure and content?*** | |
| | ***If not, what advice would you offer to make it clearer?*** | |
| **Find the thematic analysis and skim it.** | ***What are the key themes?*** | |
| | ***How are the themes further chunked out or broken down into smaller ideas?*** | |
| **Find the statement of the gap.** | ***What is the gap, and how does the proposed study address it?*** | |

**3. Free-Write/Mapping.** Free-write or map out possible questions to guide your literature review. Start with these question stems:

- What does the literature say about [problem driving your study]?
- What does the literature say about [phenomena you are interested in studying]?

**4. Scope.** Describe the scope of your study. What kind of articles or other sources will you include and why? What kind of questions will you ask to guide your search?

**5. Parameters, Inclusions, and Exclusions.** What are your search parameters? Create a list of related inclusions and exclusions to narrow your search.

**6. Drafting Search Terms.** What words will you use to search for literature? Create a "word bank" below.

**7. Keywords and Hand Searches.** Go to your library's main web page. Find the periodical locator (a search engine to locate journals). Enter a keyword that you think a journal that published in your field might contain. Browse the results. Which 3 journals do you think would be productive for you to conduct a hand search? Why?

**8. Sample Chart.** Practice analyzing an empirical study from your search using the elements of this chart.

| | |
|---|---|
| **Citation** | |
| **Study Purpose & Research Questions** | |
| **Theoretical Frame** | |
| **Methodology** | |
| **Findings** | |
| **Implications and/or Conclusions** | |
| **Limitations** | |
| **Relevance for Your Topic; Other Notes** | |
| **Relevant Quotes (with page number)** | |

**9. Initial Coding.** Using the charts you've created, start to create your initial codebook. Create a code, add an explanation of that code, and the evidence (with citations) that illustrate that code.

| INITIAL/FIRST CYCLE CODES | | |
|---|---|---|
| Code | Explanation | Illustrative Data/Citations |
| | | |
| | | |
| | | |
| | | |
| | | |
| | | |
| | | |
| | | |
| | | |

**10. Initial Coding Memos.** Based on the codes you are generating, free-write your initial coding memos: What patterns, trends, or connections are you seeing, and how do these relate to the overall problem? What evidence do you have so far that this is, indeed, a pattern?

**11. Axial Coding Organizer.** Use the organizer below to begin to create your axial codebook.

| AXIAL CODING ORGANIZER | | | |
|---|---|---|---|
| **Axial Code** | **Explanation** | **Subsumed Codes** | **Illustrative Studies/Notes** |
| | | | |
| | | | |
| | | | |
| | | | |
| | | | |
| | | | |

**12. Axial Memos.** Practice writing a category memo. Ask yourself: What is the emerging category? What is the central claim or assertion for this category? What studies illustrate these ideas? How does this category connect back to the central problem? What connections can you make to other categories or research?

**13. Theme Outline Organizer.** Use the organizer below to build out one theme, outlining its subthemes, their assertions, supporting studies, and illustrative exemplars.

**Theme 1:**

***Assertion:***

| SUBTHEME | MAIN ASSERTION(S) | SUPPORTING STUDIES | EXEMPLARS |
|---|---|---|---|
| | | | |
| | | | |
| | | | |

**14. Creating a Schema.** First, use post-its to list your major themes (one post-it per theme). Then, use the post-its to create a conceptual map or logic/process flow with your themes. How do the themes relate to each other? Is there a logical sequence, or do they form parts of a larger narrative? Then, draw out the concept map or process below. Write a sentence or two that explains the logic or overall story of the schema.

**15. Developing Level 1 Claims.** Go back to your theme organizer. The overall assertion and subtheme main assertions are your level 1 claims. Use the following organizer to evaluate them and edit as needed.

| | |
|---|---|
| **Theme 1 Assertion** | |
| **Evaluate & Revise** Theme Assertion: Does the theme claim state the overarching finding and serve as an organizing statement for your subthemes? | |
| **Subtheme Assertions** | |
| **Evaluate & Revise Subtheme Assertions:** Do the subtheme assertions unpack part of the theme and scaffold for the rest of the subsection? | |

| | |
|---|---|
| **Theme 2 Assertion** | |
| **Evaluate & Revise** Theme Assertion: Does the theme claim state the overarching finding and serve as an organizing statement for your subthemes? | |
| **Subtheme Assertions** | |
| **Evaluate & Revise Subtheme Assertions:** Do the subtheme assertions unpack part of the theme and scaffold for the rest of the subsection? | |

| | |
|---|---|
| **Theme 3 Assertion** | |
| **Evaluate & Revise** Theme Assertion: Does the theme claim state the overarching finding and serve as an organizing statement for your subthemes? | |
| **Subtheme Assertions** | |
| **Evaluate & Revise Subtheme Assertions:** Do the subtheme assertions unpack part of the theme and scaffold for the rest of the subsection? | |

**16. Drafting out Level 2 Claims.** Choose one of the subthemes from the theme you worked on above. What would be the level 2 claims? Draft at least one level 2 claim, then assess it. Do you state the number of studies? Do you make a specific claim that clearly gestures back to the subtheme level 1 claim?

**17. Drafting Out Level 3 Claims.** Working from the level 2 claim(s) you drafted, choose an exemplar from the set of studies illustrating that claim. Build out the exemplar using the organizer below.

| | |
|---|---|
| **Level 2 Claim** | |
| **Purpose of Exemplar** | |
| **Study Claim** | |
| **Relevant Methodological Details** | |

**18. Draft an Exemplar.** Use the text you generated above to draft an exemplar. Edit it together using transitions and connectors that frame the example, explicitly connect back to the level 2 claim, and states the purpose of the exemplar.

**19. Gap in Literature Exploration.** What are the gaps or shortcomings of the literature that you have analyzed? What is there not enough studies about? How does that relate to your proposed study?

**20. Generating Text for the Statement of the Gap.** Use this graphic organizer to generate text that you can edit into a paragraph or two for your statement of the gap.

| | |
|---|---|
| **Summary of what we know from the review** | |
| **Evaluative statement of extant research** | |
| **Statement of the gap** | |
| **Reminder of importance** | |
| **How your study will address the gap** | |

**21. Draft Gap Statement.** Use the text above to create a first draft of a gap statement. Edit it together using transitions and connectors, and make sure to support your claims with strategic references.

**22. Section Reflection.** Write a reflection addressing the following questions:

- What are some of your take-aways from this section?
- Did you have any "aha's" about writing a literature review?
- How did your thinking about your own study evolve during this section?
- What questions are coming up for you at this point?

# Section 6. The Theoretical Framework

**1. 3-Part Warm-up.**

**Part A.** What do you already know about theory and theoretical frameworks? What would you like to know?

**Part B.** What do you think are the purposes of a theoretical framework? What role do they play in a study?

**Part C.** Which theoretical perspectives feel most authentic to your own worldview and research interests? Why might this alignment (or tension) matter?

**2. Theory Free-Write.** What are the theories you would like to use in your project and why? If you are not sure, start with the major concepts involved in your study. Can you identify any major perspectives or theories they come from or connect to?

**3. Theory Reading and Note-Taking.** Begin building your knowledge of theory by reading relevant texts and note-taking specifically on the elements you will need to craft a theoretical framework. Choose one article and practice using the graphic organizer below.

| | |
|---|---|
| **Citation** | |
| **Definition/Purpose** | |
| **Background** | |
| **Key Concepts or Ideas** | |

**4. The Role of Theory in Empirical Research.** Search for empirical articles on your topic that use the theory or concepts you are considering. If there are not any on your topic exactly, find a few in a related area. Try out one article using the organizer below, and then continue on your own paper or computer.

| | |
|---|---|
| **Study** | |
| **Problem Framing** | |
| **Methods** | |
| **Findings and Discussion** | |

**5. Reflective Memo.** What are some of your take-aways from analyzing the way theory was "put to work" in the article you just analyzed that can be useful for your own project? How?

**6. Writing about Theory in Empirical Research.** Now, examine the theoretical writing itself in the article you read above (or another if you prefer). Use the organizer below to analyze the specific writing features of the theoretical framework.

| | |
|---|---|
| **Theory Introduction:** How do the authors first introduce their theoretical framework? What language do they use to do so? | |
| **Definition Strategies:** How do the authors define theoretical concepts (i.e., direct quotes, paraphrase, provide examples)? | |
| **Connection Language:** What specific words or phrases do the authors use to connect theory to their research problem, methods, or findings? | |
| **Criticism and Limitations:** If authors critique or acknowledge limitations, how do they write about these issues while still justifying their theoretical choices? | |
| **Voice and Positioning:** How do the authors position themselves in relation to the theory? What language choices show that relationship? | |
| **Reflection:** Which of these writing strategies would be most useful for your own theoretical framework writing? | |

**7. Preparing to Create a Theoretical Rationale**. Identify several articles from your literature review that are related in some way to your research purpose/question. Use the organizer below to record each article's citation and theoretical framework (or major concepts, models, etc). In the "memo/evaluation" column, evaluate that framework in terms of what is has added to our knowledge or helped us understand about the phenomena you are interested in (or conversely, its limitations).

| CITATION | THEORETICAL FRAMEWORK | MEMO/EVALUATION |
|---|---|---|
| | | |
| | | |
| | | |
| | | |
| | | |
| | | |
| | | |
| | | |
| | | |
| | | |

**8. Rationale Synthesis Free-Write.** Free write on the following: What trends or patterns do you see in terms of what theories or frameworks have been used to study the phenomena you are interested in? What have they helped us understand overall, and what are the major gaps?

| |
|---|
| |

**9. Building Out the Conceptual Gap Statement.** Using your notes from the summary and charts above, generate text using the prompts below.

| | |
|---|---|
| **Introductory sentence foreshadowing the conceptual gap** | |
| **Summary of the ways other researchers have conceptualized this topic** | |
| **Statement of the conceptual gap or lack, based on your assessment** | |
| **Statement of the theory you will use and how it will address this gap** | |

**10. Draft the Rationale.** Using the text you generated above, formalize your thinking into a paragraph with appropriate transitions and logical flow between sentences.

**11. Evaluating the Conceptual Gap Statement.** Now, evaluate your writing above: does this statement explicitly support the need for the theory/concepts you plan to use? Write a brief explanation of how.

**12. Exploring Theory Definition and Purpose.** Take one theory or major concept from your framework and free write: What is your theory about? What is its purpose?

**13. Writing Accessibility.** Imagine that you need to describe the same theory or concept to one of your dissertation committee members who is not familiar with it. Draft 2-3 sentences, explaining it to them.

**14. Reflect.** In the rewrite above, what did you have to adjust in your writing to make it clear? How might you take this forward into your definition for your theoretical framework?

|  |
| --- |
|  |

**15. Building Out a Theory Definition.** Use your theoretical annotations and the exercises above to generate text for your definition, using the organizer below.

| | |
| --- | --- |
| **General Definition** | |
| **Additional Details about the Theory** | |

**16. Theory Purpose Free-Write.** Jot down your thoughts on some of the purposes of your theory and how it relates to your project. Generally, what does the theory help us understand or do? What problems does it help us address?

**17. Generating Theoretical Purpose Statements the Purpose of Theory.** Use your notes above and the following stems to craft some possible purpose sentences for your theory.

- [Theory] explains...
- [Theory] helps us understand...
- [Theory] disrupts...
- [Theory] helps to think differently about...
- [Theory] helps to address [xxx issue] by...

**18. Drafting the Theory Definition and Purpose Paragraph(s).** Using notes from your readings and the text you have generated so far, write 1-2 paragraphs with:

- A definition of the theory (with enough details to get the gist of what it is)
- A discussion of the purpose of the theory (what it is meant to explain, help understand, or do)
- Citations to support your definition and purpose claims

**19. Theory Background Free-Write.** Free-write for 5 minutes on the following prompt: What do you know about your theory's background (e.g., where it comes from, important theorists, developments over time)?

**20. Generating Ideas and Text for the Theory Background.** Bullet out information in response to the prompts below.

| | |
|---|---|
| **Theory Roots** | |
| **Key Theorists** | |
| **Theory Evolution** | |
| **Differing Perspectives** | |
| **Critiques, Controversies, or other Background** | |
| **Anything Specific to your Topic** | |

**21. Writing a Draft of the Theory Background**. Using your notes from the graphic organizer above, craft a paragraph or two for your background. Make sure that you can identify the purpose of each sentence (i.e., the component of the background it addresses).

**22. Exploring Major Concepts.** Free-write on the following: What major concepts are you considering including in your theoretical framework? Why?

**23. Concept Mapping Your Theory.** Before diving into formal definitions, create a simple concept map below. Put your main theory in the center, then draw lines to its most important concepts. For each concept, jot down 2-3 words that come to mind when you think about it.

**24. Concept Logic Flow.** List all the theoretical concepts you think you might need to discuss. Now arrange them in order from most fundamental (i.e., readers need to understand this first) to most specific (i.e., builds on other concepts). How might this help you think about the logical order for presenting concepts in your writing?

**26. Concept Connections.** Before you start building out your concept paragraphs, you also want to think through the overall connections, purposes, and alignment. For each major concept, complete these sentences:

- This concept relates to [another concept in my framework] by...
- This concept helps explain [aspect of my research problem] because...
- This concept will be important for understanding my findings when...

**27. Building Out a Concept.** Use your notes and the free-write to generate text for one of your concepts using the organizer below.

| **CONCEPT:** | |
|---|---|
| **Sentence that introduces the concept** | |
| **Definition and other important details** | |
| **Examples that contextualize the concept** | |
| **How this concept connects to other concepts in your framework** | |
| **One key quote from a theorist that captures this concept** | |
| **How the concept will be used in your study** | |

**28. Editing into a Cohesive Subsection.** Edit the notes above into 1-3 paragraphs that build out the key concept subsection, with appropriate references. Be sure to use transitions, signaling language, and other scaffolds to support your reader. Then, repeat this activity with each major concept you plan to use in your study.

**31. Concept Synthesis**. Write a 3-4 sentence paragraph that explains how all your major concepts work together to form a coherent framework. This "synthesis paragraph" can help you see gaps in logic and identify where you need stronger connections between concepts. You can also use this paragraph as a conclusion.

**32. Chapter Reflection.** Write a reflection addressing the following questions:

- What are some of your take-aways from this chapter?
- Did you have any "aha's"? How will these affect your theoretical frame development and writing?
- How has your understanding of theory's role in research developed through these activities?
- How are your problem statement, literature review, and emerging theoretical framework aligned? What areas that might need further examination?
- What questions are coming up for you at this point?

# Section 7. The Methodology Chapter

**1. 2-Part Warm-up.**

**Part A.** What do you already know about the methodology chapter of the dissertation proposal or dissertation itself? What do you need to learn more about? What questions or concerns do you have regarding this chapter?

**Part B.** What are your current thoughts your research design? Based on your research question, what are possible avenues you might take?

**2. Anatomy of a Methodology Chapter.** Find a dissertation in your area with a methodological approach similar to the one you are thinking about taking. Find the methodology chapter, identify its major sections (denoted by headings), and record them in the lefthand column. In the righthand column, describe what elements you find in that section and their content.

| MAJOR SECTION | SECTION PURPOSE & CONTENT |
|---|---|
| | |
| | |
| | |
| | |
| | |
| | |

**3. Methodology Chapter Reflection.** How are the major elements included in this chapter similar to or different from those laid out at the beginning of chapter 7 of STLOP? If there were different sections, do you think they might be relevant for your study? What are your overall takeaways from this activity regarding what types of information to include in a methods section?

**4. Methodology Free-Write.** What is your current thinking in terms of your overall research approach (quantitative, qualitative, mixed methods, arts-based, etc)? Explain your reasoning.

**5. Positioning Yourself Methodologically.** Look back at your problem statement and research questions. Write a reflection on the following: What assumptions about knowledge and reality (i.e., onto-epistemology) are embedded in how you've framed your study? Do these align best with a positivist, post-positivist, critical, or post-foundational stance? How might that inform your methodological choices?

**6. General Methodological Approach Exploration.** Bullet out your thoughts for each element. First, think through the general approach and its major characteristics, as well as how it aligns with and supports your theoretical frame and study goals. Then, do the same with the specific onto-epistemological stance you will identified above.

| | APPROACH DEFINITION AND DETAILS | THEORETICAL ALIGNMENT | SUPPORT FOR STUDY GOALS |
|---|---|---|---|
| **General Approach** | | | |
| **Onto-Epistemological Stance** | | | |

**7. General Methodological Approach Draft**: Use the notes you generated above to draft one or two paragraphs that describe your general methodological approach and situates your study in a specific onto-epistemological stance. Remember to use topic sentences, signaling language, transitions, and other scaffolds for coherence and to support the reader's understanding.

**8. Thinking through Participant Information.** Bullet out information to include in your participant section in terms of specific demographics, background/experience, and/or any other information relevant for your study. Then, write a justification: why do you need participants with these characteristics?

| | |
|---|---|
| **Demographics** | |
| **Background or Experience** | |
| **Other Relevant Information** | |
| **Justification for the Above** | |

**9. Thinking through the Setting.** Jot down information about your research study setting (if appropriate). Consider: what would your reader need to know about where the study will take or took place to make sense of the findings?

**10. Adding Additional Context.** Do you need to add any additional contextual information, such as interventions, programs, or descriptions of other elements important to the study? Bullet out this additional context out below.

**11. Rough Draft of Participants/Context Section.** Draft out your participants and context subsection. Use the text you generated in the previous pre-writing exercises to develop it into paragraphs. Then, evaluate your writing for specificity and detail.

**12. Data Collection Free-Write.** What kinds of data are you going to collect to answer your research question(s)? Why? What do you think each type of data source will do for you in relation to your research questions?

**13. Data Source-Question Alignment.** Use the graphic organizer below to explore the alignment between your planned data sources and your research question(s). Add your research questions at the top and your data sources to the lefthand column. Then articulate how each data source will help you "answer" each question.

| DATA SOURCE | RESEARCH QUESTION 1: | RESEARCH QUESTION 2: |
|---|---|---|
| | | |
| | | |
| | | |
| | | |

**14. Thinking Through Data Sources.** Choose one data source and use the chart below to think through each of the elements and generate text for writing its description. Then, use the chart as a template and create one for each kind of data source.

| | DATA SOURCE: |
|---|---|
| Definition | |
| Important Methodologists | |
| Contextualization to Your Study | |
| Tradition of Origin | |
| Connected Concepts/Ideas | |
| Associated Tools, Materials, or Processes | |

**15. Thinking through Data Collection Logistics.** Using the same data source as above, think through each of the elements in the organizer below and generate text for writing the description. Then, use the table as a template and create one for each kind of data source, as you did above.

| | DATA SOURCE: |
|---|---|
| **Who** | |
| **When** | |
| **Where** | |
| **How Many** | |
| **How Long** | |
| **Other Details** | |

**16. Example Analysis.** Read the paragraph describing the logistics of a data source. What kinds of concrete details are provided?

*My total number of observations varied for each teacher. Because I was interested in the construction of practice, I made the decision to observe each study participant for the length of one instructional unit, so that I might see several consecutive lessons that supported a larger learning objective. For June and Mauro, whose classes were eighty-minute periods, this meant I observed seven and five classes, respectively. However, for Bruce, whose classes were only forty minutes, one unit spanned ten classes. In addition to the complete unit, I observed each teacher two to three times in September, as their schedules allowed, to get an understanding of classroom dynamics. Finally, I observed a "mini-unit," which consisted of three to four classes for each teacher, toward the end of the first semester, to note any additional changes or developments that might have taken place since the observed unit. Because each class is a unique composition of the teacher, students, content, forces, and objects that can shape what the teacher can do, I planned my data collection schedule to observe as many different periods as time allowed.*

**17. At-A-Glance Data Source Chart.** If you have multiple types of data, use the table below to create an at-a-glance data source chart to add to your data source section.

| DATA SOURCE | DESCRIPTION | NUMBER |
|---|---|---|
| | | |
| | | |
| | | |
| | | |

**17. Data Source Draft.** Use the text you generated in the activities above to craft paragraphs for your data sources draft. If you have more than one type of data source, chunk them into subsections with subheadings clearly labeling each one. Then, evaluate your writing:

- What kind of language did you use to help readers concretely visualize your data collection process? How could you strengthen it?
- How effectively did you use scaffolds like subheadings , topic sentences, and signaling phrases to organize complex procedural information? What edits could you make to improve this dimension?

**19. Data Source Rationale.** Imagine a skeptical committee member asks: "Why did you choose this particular data collection method?" Write a response that explains your thinking, showing how your data collection choices support your research goals.

**20. Data Collection Reflection.** What might be some possible challenges or complications for collecting the data you have described above? How might you adapt if your data collection doesn't unfold as planned?

**21. Generating Text for the Analysis Section.** Use the chart below to through your general analysis, jotting down the approach, its definition, and a justification explaining why you have chosen that analysis method. If you have a combination of approaches, complete a row for each method of analysis you plan to use.

| APPROACH | DEFINITION | JUSTIFICATION |
|---|---|---|
| | | |
| | | |
| | | |

**22. Fleshing Out Steps for Analysis.** Outline the process you plan to take to conduct your analysis, step by step. "Name" each step according to the analytic approach you and your advisor have settled on and describe it in the middle column. Add any methodological concepts and definitions for that step (for example, "focused coding"). Make sure you add citations where necessary.

| STEP | DETAILED DESCRIPTION | CONCEPT DEFINITIONS |
|---|---|---|
| | | |
| | | |
| | | |
| | | |

**23. Analysis Section Draft.** Using your notes from the two activities above, draft out paragraphs for the two parts of your analysis section: the discussion of the analytic approach and the detailed description of specific steps you plan to take. Make sure to use sequencing language ("first," "next," "finally") and other scaffolds to support your reader's understanding.

**24. Coherence Web.** Create a visual map showing connections between your theoretical framework, research questions, methodological approach, specific data sources, and analysis plan. Where are the connections strongest? Where might you need to strengthen the alignment?

**25. Trustworthiness Text Generation.** Below, write out your definition of trustworthiness, along with appropriate citations. If you are drawing form multiple definitions, bullet them out. Then, think through and generate a list of trustworthiness quality criteria from this definition.

| **Definition of Trustworthiness** | |
|---|---|
| **Corresponding Quality Criteria** | |

**27. Thinking Through Trustworthiness Criteria.** Taking the criteria you identified from the previous activity, use the organizer below to develop trustworthiness strategies that correspond to each criterion and build out text for writing the description.

| CRITERION | MEASURE(S) TO ADDRESS CRITERION |
| --- | --- |
| | |
| | |
| | |
| | |
| | |

**28. Trustworthiness Draft.** Using the ideas you generated in the last two exercises, edit into 1-2 paragraphs.

**29. Positionality Mapping Exercise.** Think through your positionality using the prompts of identity factors below. If there are other salient factors that influence your positionality, add them in the blank spaces.

| | |
|---|---|
| **Current Role/ Context** | |
| **Beliefs Related to Your Topic** | |
| **Interests and Professional Goals** | |
| **Personal Experiences and Background** | |
| **Professional Experiences and Background** | |
| **Theoretical/Onto-Epistemological orientations** | |
| | |
| | |

**30. Thinking Through Potential Impact of Positionality.** Using the previous activity, select several of the positionality elements that you think could be relevant for your study. Then, using the righthand column, think through ways that this positionality might impact a facet of the study in some way (whether positively or negatively)—such as the framing of the study, data collection, access to participants, your interpretations, and so on.

| POSITIONALITY ELEMENT | POSSIBLE IMPACT |
|---|---|
| | |
| | |
| | |
| | |
| | |

**31. Power Analysis.** Which of the positionalities above might have implications in terms of power dynamics between you and your participants—or any other dimension of the study? How will you address any potential power differentials?

**32. Drafting the Initial Positionality/Reflexivity Section.** Using the notes you generated from the previous three activities, draft an initial positionality/reflexivity section that describes salient dimensions of your positionality (including contextual factors), ways that those have or might impact the project, and any power implications.

**33. Proposal Abstract Structure.** Complete the sentence stems.

| | |
|---|---|
| **The problem/issue is...** | |
| **This is a problem/ important because ...** | |
| **Researchers who have studied this problem have found ...** | |
| **We still don't know ...** | |
| **Therefore, I am going to investigate ...** | |
| **I will use a theoretical frame of ...** | |
| **I will conduct the study using ... [methodology]** | |
| **The central question(s) guiding this study is/ are...** | |

**34. Proposal Abstract Draft.** Put the sentences into paragraph form, edit out unnecessary language, and add transitions for flow.

**35. Reflection.** Write a reflection addressing the following questions:

- What are some of your take-aways from this section?
- Did you have any "aha's" about writing about research designs?
- What insights about organizing complex methodological information and scaffolding reader understanding do you plan to use?
- Which aspects of methodology writing feel most manageable now versus still needing focused attention and practice?
- What questions are coming up for you at this point?

# Section 8. The Findings Chapter

**1. Warm-Up.** What do you think the purpose of a findings chapter is, in your own words? What will be *your* specific goals in this chapter?

**2. Analyzing a Sample Findings Chapter, Part A.** Locate a dissertation in your topic area that uses a similar methodology as you used. Go to the findings chapter (usually chapter 4). Create an outline that shows the organization and key findings.

**3. Analyzing a Sample Findings Chapter, Part B.** What do you notice about the organization of the findings? How would you describe it? Is it effective for communicating the outcomes of the study? Why or why not?

**4. Articulating Big Ideas.** Based on your analysis so far, what is your current thinking regarding how your emerging findings shed light on your research question(s)? (No need to look at your analysis; write off the top of your head.)

**5. Keeping the Big Picture in Mind.** Complete this sentence: "By the time my reader finishes my findings chapter, the most important thing I want them to understand is..."

**6. Schema Pre-Write: Relationships between Ideas.** What are the big ideas that have emerged from your analysis? Is there a story or narrative emerging? How do these ideas relate to each other?

**7. Schema Exploration.** Begin exploring a schema for your findings by creating a concept map with the ideas you identified above. Draw lines to indicate relationships between ideas.

**8. Creating Multiple Schemas.** Take your main findings and experiment with organizing them in different ways. Choose few approaches below, then reflect on how effective that organizational structure is.

- ***By Research Question:*** Organize findings by directly addressing each research question in order.
- ***By Level of Significance:*** Organize from most to least important findings, or from broad patterns to specific details.
- ***By Process or Development Over Time:*** Organize findings chronologically to show how something unfolds, develops, or changes.
- ***By Theoretical Framework Components:*** Organize findings around the key concepts or elements of your theoretical framework.
- ***By Themes with Subthemes:*** Organize findings into major themes, each with supporting sub-themes.

| Schema 1 | Evaluation: |
| --- | --- |
| | |

| Schema 2 | Evaluation: |
| --- | --- |
| | |

| **Schema 3** | **Evaluation:** |
| --- | --- |
| | |

**9. Schema Justification Exercise.** Once you have chosen your schema, practice articulating why this organizational approach best serves your study. This will help you make deliberate choices about structure.

| | |
|---|---|
| **Chosen schema:** | |
| **Why this schema fits your methodology:** | |
| **How this schema will help your reader understand your findings:** | |

**10. "Answering" Study Questions, Part A.** Record your themes or big ideas from your chapter 4 in the lefthand column. Then, think through how that theme/idea connects back to or "answers" one or more of your study questions.

| THEME | HOW IT CONNECTS TO RESEARCH QUESTIONS |
|---|---|
| | |
| | |
| | |
| | |

**11. "Answering" Study Questions, Part B.** Now, create a 1-2 sentence overall summary of how the big ideas answer your questions, using the text generated to help you.

| **Summary:** |
|---|
| |

**12. Crafting an Overall Findings Assertion**. Create a draft of your overall findings assertion (a high-level summary of your analysis). Then, evaluate it using the criteria on the right and revise accordingly.

| **Overall Assertion:** | |
|---|---|
| **Revision:** Is the assertion specific? Does it add knowledge? Does it connect to patterns? | |

**13. Crafting Theme Assertions.** Record your main themes or ideas in the lefthand column. Then create claims for each of your themes. Make sure they are specific, add knowledge, and connect to patterns.

| THEME/IDEA | ASSERTION |
|---|---|
| | |
| | |
| | |
| | |

**14. Analyzing Paragraph-Level Claims and Evidence.** Read the excerpt below. What paragraph-level claims are made? What evidence is presented to support them?

*As she indicated in her first interview and subsequent lesson debriefs, June believed that many of her students had internalized the label of "special needs" and lacked confidence in their academic abilities, which often resulted in "shutting down" or refusing to engage in particular academic tasks. I observed that such student response was particularly acute during summative or "high stakes" assessments. When a student "shut down," June simply tried to find other ways to help him or her, either by modifying the section of the exam with which the student was struggling, rephrasing her questions, or further scaffolding his or her work in some way. For example, when students were unable to complete a section of a formal assessment that asked for the definition of terms relating to the scientific method, June wrote the definitions on the paper and asked them to match the word to their definitions. (Strom, 2014, 239-240)*

**15. Analyzing Writing about Evidence.** Go back and read the paragraph above again. What are the ways that language is used to present evidence? How does this help support the reader to follow the unfolding ideas?

**16. Evidence and Analytic Explanation.** Read the example. Can you identify the paragraph-level claims? What evidence is presented? How does the evidence support the claims made? What kinds of analytic explanation is included? In what ways does it help the reader to understand the evidence and/or interpret it?

*As June spent more time with her students, she began differentiating her negotiation strategies, learning that what worked with one student did not necessarily work with another. Some students responded consistently to a particular incentive or strategy, and thus she could rely on a specific tactic to work the majority of the time. By way of example, June explained, "[Student's name] responds really well to feeling successful. So if she feels that she's doing a great job, or that she's really smart, she'll keep pushing herself." When working with this student, June would continually remind her how well she was doing during class activities. She also maintained frequent contact with her mother, texting her often about the student's accomplishments. Other students were not as predictable, but she used her knowledge of them to determine a course of action. For example, she recognized that another student's needed to be in constant motion, and modified her instructional plans accordingly. During a class exploring the structure of water molecules, June named the student her assistant, directing him to draw accompanying visuals for the lesson and make appropriate notations on the board throughout the class. Explaining her thinking with regard to engaging the student in the learning activity, June articulated, "He can't help it, he needs to be moving...so who did I have at the board the entire time? [Student's name]. 'Can you write this, can you draw this? Can you do this?'" As June learned more about her students' needs and strengths, she was able to individualize her teaching strategies for them and achieved higher rates of participation in instruction, which in turn supported her enactment of practices that were learner-centered and involved cognitively challenging tasks, like scientific reasoning. (Strom, 2014, 249-250)*

**17. Distinguishing Analytic Description from Interpretation.** Read the examples of assertions below and note whether they are descriptive or analytic. Explain how you know.

| | DESCRIPTIVE OR INTERPRETIVE? | HOW DO YOU KNOW? |
|---|---|---|
| All participants mentioned feeling overwhelmed during their first month of teaching. | | |
| Participants' consistent reports of feeling overwhelmed speak to a disconnect between their preservice preparation and daily realities. | | |
| The data showed three main themes related to teacher identity. | | |
| Teachers' shifting language about their role suggests that identity development occurs through practice rather than prior to it. | | |

**18. Discussing Evidence.** Choose one piece of evidence—perhaps a compelling quote, example, or vignette. Then, brainstorm related description and interpretation, using the prompts below.

| | |
|---|---|
| **Evidence** | |
| **What does it show?** | |
| **How do you plan to use it?** | |
| **What is most compelling about this evidence?** | |
| **What larger study patterns, complexities, arguments, or impacts does it relate to?** | |

**19. Practicing Writing about Evidence.** Write a few sentences that discusses the piece of evidence from the last activity. How will you introduce the evidence? How will you make the purpose of the evidence and its connection to bigger patterns/ points clear to your reader? Experiment with a few different ways of writing about it and assess them for effectiveness.

**20. Combining Claim, Evidence, and Analysis.** Choose one subtheme or smaller section from your study to build out. Take one key idea from that subtheme/section and turn it into a paragraph-level claim. Then, bullet out your thoughts on what kind of further unpacking or description your reader needs to understand the claim; add evidence that supports the claim; and brainstorm an interpretation that helps the reader understand what that evidence means and how it supports the paragraph-level claim.

| **Subtheme** | |
|---|---|
| **Paragraph-Level Claim** | |
| **Analytic Description** | |
| **Evidence** | |
| **Analytic Interpretation** | |

**22. Deepening Interpretation.** Using the claim and interpretation of the evidence above, practice pushing your interpretation beyond surface description, brainstorming each level below.

| **Claim:** | |
|---|---|
| **Evidence:** | |
| **Surface:** What happened? | |
| **Pattern:** What does this represent? | |
| **Explanation:** Why might this pattern exist? | |
| **Significance:** What are the broader implications? | |

**23. Comparing Interpretations Exercise**. Analysis is a situated practice, and there are often multiple ways to interpret evidence. Take one interpretation and consider at least two other possible ways of understanding the related evidence. Then, evaluate them all in terms of which is the most supported.

| **Your Primary Interpretation:** | |
|---|---|
| **Alternative Interpretation 1:** | |
| **Alternative Interpretation 2:** | |
| **Most Supported Interpretation, and Why** | |

**24. Building out a Draft Findings Paragraph.** Using the last several activities, write a draft paragraph from your findings. Ensure that you have a paragraph-level claim with description, evidence, and interpretation.

**25. Scaffolding for the Reader.** Read your draft paragraph, above, and identify places where 1) you need more specificity, precision, details, and/or elaboration for the reader to be able to follow along; and 2) you can add signaling language and transitions that make clear the relationships between ideas. Then, revise the paragraph below.

**26. Generating Text for Your Findings Introduction.** Use the organizer below to craft out your big ideas/aha's and a roadmap.

| | |
|---|---|
| **Major ideas/Aha's:** Bullet out the major takeaways of your findings as a whole | |
| **Road Map:** Bullet out the headings of your findings schema, with brief explanations if needed. | |

**27. Crafting a Cohesive Findings Introduction.** Edit your work from the previous activity into a 1-2 paragraph introduction to your findings. Don't forget transitions!

**29. Chapter Reflection.** Write a reflection addressing the following questions:

- What are some of your take-aways from this section?
- Did you have any "aha's" about writing the findings?
- What questions are coming up for you at this point?
- How has your understanding of the difference between reporting data and presenting findings evolved? What about description and interpretation?
- What aspects of crafting your findings chapter do you feel most confident about? What do you still need to work on?

# Section 9. The Discussion and Recommendations

**1. Warm-up:** Imagine that you are giving a presentation on your study to a group of practitioners or professionals in your field who do not have a research background. What points would you highlight in terms of 1) why the findings are important and 2) how findings can concretely inform their work?

**2. Purposes of the Discussion.** What are the purposes of the discussion, in your own words? What are your goals for this chapter?

**3. Discussion Chapter Analysis.** Analyze the discussion chapter (typically chapter 5) of a selected dissertation to determine how the author addressed the following:

| | |
|---|---|
| **Overall organization of the chapter** | |
| **Interpretation of findings through theory** | |
| **Discussion of how findings compare to previous research** | |
| **Implications or applications for policy, practice, and/or research** | |
| **Recommendations for action based on findings** | |

**4. Discussion Analysis Reflection.** Based on your analysis of the sample dissertation's discussion chapter, what did you notice about how that author handled the discussion that you want to emulate in your own writing? What did you notice that you want to do differently?

**5. Discussion Chapter Planning.** Before diving into writing, reflect on the overall story you want to tell in your discussion. Use these sentence frames to get started if needed:

- *The most surprising thing I learned from this study was...*
- *The most important thing for my field to understand from this study is...*
- *If I could change one thing about practice/policy based on my findings, it would be...*
- *The biggest question my study raises for future research is...*

**6. Generating Ideas for Conclusions.** List your major findings (i.e., your themes) in the lefthand column. Then, jot down your thoughts on 1) the big aha's from that finding and 2) what is important about that understanding, or what we can learn from it.

| FINDING | BIG AHA'S | IMPORTANCE/LEARNING |
|---|---|---|
| | | |
| | | |
| | | |
| | | |

**7. Crafting Conclusions.** Use the text you generated above to draft at least one major conclusion per finding. For each conclusion, what are the major points to be made, and what examples from the findings support them?

**8. Outlining Conclusion Paragraphs.** Using the organizer, take one conclusion you have decided on and break it down into claims, along with explanation and evidence (examples from your findings).

| Main conclusion: | | |
|---|---|---|
| Claim 1 | Explanation | Evidence |
| Claim 2 | Explanation | Evidence |
| Claim 3 | Explanation | Evidence |

**9. Drafting One Conclusion Discussion.** Draft the work above into one section of your discussion. Remember to use transitions, reference examples from your findings, and avoid absolute language.

**10. Avoiding Overstatement.** Review the conclusion discussion above. Circle any absolute language (words like "all," "never," "always," "proves," "definitely"). Revise as needed to temper your statements, using qualifier language like "suggests," "indicates," "appears," "tends to," or "in this context."

**11. Connecting to Research Quick Write.** Off the top of your head, how do your findings compare to the major ideas in your literature review? What are the areas of similarity and difference? Are there any ideas that came up that *aren't* included in your literature review?

**12. Surfacing Findings-Literature Relationships, Part 1.** Bullet out 1) the main ideas from your literature review, 2) then your main findings, then 3) your main discussion conclusions.

| Main Ideas from Literature Review | |
|---|---|
| Main Findings from Your Study | |
| Your Conclusions | |

**13. Surfacing Findings-Literature Relationships, Part 2.** Looking across the three columns above, what relationships do you see? Which findings confirm, extend, contradict, or nuance prior research? Jot your thoughts below.

**14. Articulating Specific Literature Connections.** Using the previous activity, distill the specific findings/conclusions that you found connections for. Write brief summaries of your findings/conclusions. In the righthand column, draft out a description of the connection, with matching citations.

| FINDINGS/CONCLUSION | CONNECTION TO PREVIOUS RESEARCH |
| --- | --- |
| | |
| | |
| | |
| | |
| | |

**15. Literature Connection Starters.** Practice introducing connections to prior research using varied language. Below are several sentence starters to use. Experiment with your own as well.

- "These findings align with [Author's] argument that..."
- "While [Author] found [X], this study suggests..."
- "Building on [Author's] work, these findings indicate..."
- "This study provides additional support for [Author's] claim that..."

**16. Surfacing Empirical Contributions.** Looking at the connections you have provided, what are the empirical contributions you can highlight (the new or different understandings your original data analysis offers)?

**17. Drafting a Paragraph of Literature Connections.** Using the ideas you generated from the last several activities, choose one finding/conclusion and build out a paragraph discussing its connections to the literature and empirical contributions. Remember to cite your sources and connect to specific examples from your findings to illustrate the connections.

**18. Theorizing Findings Free-Write.** What aha's have you had so far that relate to your theoretical framework? How has your theoretical framework, or related concepts, helped you understand your study findings or their significance?

**19. Making Theoretical Connections.** Summarize your major findings/conclusions on the left; in the righthand column, jot down how you might use your theoretical framework (or parts of it) to interpret each of them. If you are not sure, write down any connections between the finding and the theory/ concept that you can think of.

| FINDING/CONCLUSION | THEORETICAL INTERPRETATION |
|---|---|
| | |
| | |
| | |
| | |

**20. Building Out Theoretical Discussion.** Using the structure of an argument (claim, explanation, evidence) choose one finding/theoretical interpretation pair from above and build out text for your discussion of that specific interpretation.

| Finding and Theoretical Interpretation | |
|---|---|
| Theoretical Claim | |
| Explanation of the Theorization and Significance | |
| Examples that Support the Theorization | |

**21. Reflection on Theorizing.** Assess the interpretation you just wrote: How does your theoretical interpretation help explain why this finding occurred, or get to the "so what"? What specific concepts from your framework are you drawing on, and how do they help illuminate this finding?

**22. Identifying Theoretical Contributions.** Copy over the main gist of each of your theoretical interpretations. For each interpretation, brainstorm what the contribution is (e.g., how it helps us do or understand something differently).

| THEORETICAL INTERPRETATION | THEORETICAL CONTRIBUTIONS |
|---|---|
| | |
| | |
| | |
| | |

**23. Articulating the "So What" of Theoretical Contributions.** Free-write: why are the theoretical contributions you named above important? What are their practical implications?

**23. Writing Contribution Statements**. Practice writing clear, confident contribution statements. Complete these sentence frames using the text you generated above, and experiment with some additional frames of your own.

- *"This study contributes to [field/literature area] by..."*
- *"These findings advance our understanding of [phenomenon] by demonstrating..."*
- *"This research fills a gap in [area] by providing evidence that..."*

**24. Draft a Theoretical Interpretation Paragraph.** Use the text you generated in the last several activities to craft one paragraph of theoretical discussion. Present the interpretation along with explanation and illustration with your own data, cite appropriate theoretical sources, and articulate the theoretical contribution.

| What kinds of language choices did you make in this theoretical interpretation, and how do they support your reader? | |
|---|---|

**25. Plotting out your discussion.** I find it very helpful to plan out my writing in advance. This organizer helps you think through your introduction, organize your discussion into sections (each unpacking a major conclusion), and plot out the examples, connections to literature, and connections to theory (theorizations) for each.

| Intro | Brief summary of findings | |
|---|---|---|
| | Summary of discussion structure | |

| **Conclusion 1** | |
|---|---|
| **Main points to unpack this conclusion** | |
| **Examples to support conclusion** | |
| **Connections to literature** | |
| **Connections to theory** | |

| | |
|---|---|
| **Conclusion 2** | |
| **Main points to unpack this conclusion** | |
| **Examples to support conclusion** | |
| **Connections to literature** | |
| **Connections to theory** | |

| **Conclusion 3** | |
|---|---|
| **Main points to unpack this conclusion** | |
| **Examples to support conclusion** | |
| **Connections to literature** | |
| **Connections to theory** | |

**26. Coherence Check.** Read through your discussion outline and evaluate using the following:

| | |
|---|---|
| **Does each section flow logically to the next?** | |
| **Have I repeated myself anywhere?** | |
| **Does my discussion feel balanced between findings?** | |
| **What is the overall "story" I am telling?** | |

**27. Scaffolding Language Practice.** Draft transitions between your major discussion sections using road mapping and signaling language, such as the following:

- "Having established [X], I now turn to..."
- "The second major implication concerns..."
- "While the previous section focused on [X], this section examines..."

| | |
|---|---|
| **Transition between sections 1-2** | |
| **Transition between sections 2-3** | |
| **Transition between sections 3-4** | |

**28. Recommendations Warm-Up.** What groups of stakeholders are your findings relevant for? That is, who would benefit from learning about the lessons your findings provide? List as many as you can think of.

**29. Stakeholder Prioritization.** Now, prioritize the groups you identified, above. Which 2-3 groups would benefit most from your findings? Which groups have the most power to implement changes based on your recommendations?

**30. Plotting Recommendations, Part 1.** Plot out one set of recommendations that flow from your findings for a specific stakeholder group. Name the stakeholder group, then add the finding/conclusion that the recommendation flows from. Finally, brainstorm what types of recommendations you will make generally: policy, practice, research training, professional development, etc.

| | |
|---|---|
| **Stakeholder Group** | |
| **Connected Finding** | |
| **Kind of Recommendations** | |

**31. Plotting Recommendations, Part 2.** Now, sketch out the lesson(s) for the stakeholder group on the left, and a specific action they could take on the right.

| Recommendation: Suggestion | Recommendation: Actionable Item |
|---|---|
| | |
| | |
| | |

**32. Drafting a Recommendation.** Using the organizer above, move the set of recommendations into paragraph form. Then, assess them for the following:

- Have you clearly labeled the stakeholder group?
- How do you let the reader know what finding/conclusion this set of recommendations comes from?
- Does each individual recommendation in this set have a more general suggestion accompanied by a concrete, actionable item to put that suggestion into practice?
- What scaffolds do you use, and how do they support the reader's understanding?

**33. Future Research Integration.** Often recommendations for future research feel like an afterthought. Instead, consider how might future research directions connect to your other recommendations. What research would need to happen to support the policy or practice changes you're suggesting?

**34. Dissertation Conclusion Quick Write.** You are standing in an elevator with a highly respected researcher from your field and introduce yourself. This scholar is very interested in learning about your study, but you only have until they get to the top floor to tell them about it! Come up with a thirty-second soundbite highlighting the most important pieces of information from your dissertation to share.

**36. Conclusion Text Generation.** Think through the following prompts for your conclusion and bullet out your thoughts.

| | |
|---|---|
| **Summarize your project and its goals.** | |
| **Are there any particularly powerful findings you want to emphasize?** | |
| **Restate your argument about the need to solve the problem you originally posed.** | |
| **List the most important contributions of the paper and how they will help mediate the problem.** | |
| **What uplifting or hopeful thought could you leave your reader with?** | |

**37. Drafting the Conclusion.** Using the last two activities, write a draft of your conclusion. Then assess: does it summarize your most important findings, major argument, and most important contributions? How does it support the reader to follow your final thoughts?

**38. Final Reflection.** Write a reflection addressing the following questions:

- What was most challenging about moving from describing your findings to interpreting their significance? What was challenging about using those findings and interpretations to make concrete suggestions for change?
- How did writing the discussion change your understanding of your own study?
- What advice would you give to someone else about writing a discussion chapter?
- What questions are you still grappling with as you finish this chapter?

# References


Altheide, D., & Johnson, D. (2011). Reflections on interpretive adequacy in qualitative research. In N. Denzin & Y. Lincoln (Eds.), *The sage handbook of qualitative research, 4th ed.,* pp. 581-594. Sage.

Bennett, J. (2009). *Vibrant matter: A political ecology of things.* Duke University Press.

Bergeron, B. (2008). Enacting a culturally responsive curriculum in a novice teacher's classroom: Encountering disequilibrium. *Urban Education, 43*(4), 4-28.

Birrell, J. (1995). Learning how the game is played: A beginning teacher's struggle to prepare Black youth for a white world. *Teaching and Teacher Education, 11*(2), 137-147.

Braidotti, R. (2006). Posthuman, all too human: Towards a new process ontology. *Theory, culture & society, 23*(7-8), 197-208.

Braidotti, R. (2013). *The posthuman.* Polity Press.

Brashier, A. & Norris, E. (2008). Breaking down barriers for first year teachers: What teacher education preparation programs can do. *Journal of Early Childhood Teacher Education, 29*(1), 30-44.

Butz, M. R. (1997). *Chaos and complexity: Implications for psychological theory and practice.* Taylor & Francis.

Byrne, D. (1998). *Complexity theory and the social sciences.* Routledge.

Chirichello, M. (2001, January). *Preparing principals to lead in the new millennium: A response to the leadership crisis in American schools.* Paper presented at the International Congress for School Effectiveness and Improvement, Toronto, Canada.

Clarke, A., & Collins, S. (2007). Complexity science and student teacher supervision. Teaching and Teacher Education, 23, 160–172.

Cochran-Smith, M., Ell, F., Ludlow, L., Grudnoff, L., & Aitken, G. (2014). The challenge and promise of complexity theory for teacher education research. *Teachers College Record, 116*(4), 1-38.

Coffey, H., & Farinde-Wu, A. (2016). Navigating the journey to culturally responsive teaching: Lessons from the success and struggles of one first-year, Black female teacher of Black students in an urban school. *Teaching and Teacher Education, 60,* 24-33.

Cook, J. (2009). "Coming into my own as a teacher": Identity, disequilibrium, and the first year of teaching. *The New Educator, 5*(4), 274-292.

Davis, B., & Sumara, D. (1997). Cognition, complexity, and teacher education. *Harvard educational review, 67*(1), 105-126.

Davis, B., & Sumara, D. (2006). *Complexity and education: Inquiries into learning, teaching and research.* Lawrence Erlbaum.

de Freitas, E. (2012). Classroom as rhizome: New strategies for diagramming knotted interactions. *Qualitative Inquiry, 18*(7), 557-570.

Deleuze, G., & Guattari, F. (1987). *Capitalism and schizophrenia: A thousand plateaus.* University of Minnesota Press.

Denzin, K. & Lincoln, Y. S. (2005). *The Sage handbook of qualitative research, 3rd Ed.* Sage.

Ellsworth, E. (1989). Why doesn't this feel empowering? Working through repressive myths of critical pedagogy. *Harvard Educational Review 59*(3), 297-324.

Esparo, L. J., & Rader, R. (2001). The leadership crisis: The shortage of qualified superintendents is not going away. *American School Board Journal, 188*(5), 46-48.

Fullan, M. (2003). *Change forces with a vengeance.* RoutledgeFalmer.

Giroux, H. A. (1992). Educational leadership and the crisis of democratic government. *Educational Researcher, 21*(4), 4-11.

Leavy, P. (2014). Introduction. In P. Leavy (Ed.), *The Oxford handbook of qualitative research* (pp. 1–14). Oxford University Press.

Leavy, P. (2017). *Research design: Quantitative, qualitative, mixed methods, arts-based, and community-based participatory research approaches.* Guilford.

Malone, B. G., & Caddell, T. (2000). A crisis in leadership: Where are tomorrow's principals? *Clearing House, 73*(3), 162-164.

Mason, M. (2008). Complexity theory and the philosophy of education. In M. Mason (Ed.), *Complexity theory and the philosophy of education* (pp. 46–61). Wiley-Blackwell.

Maxcy, S. J. (1994). *Postmodern school leadership: Meeting the crisis in educational administration.* Praeger Publishers.

Merriam S. (2009). *Qualitative research: A guide to design and implementation* (3rd ed.). Jossey-Bass.

National Council for Accreditation of Teacher Educators (NCATE). (2001). Standards for professional development schools. Retrieved on 6/12/2024 from http:www.ncate.org/documents/pdsstandards.pdf

Newman, E. (2010). 'I'm being measured as an NQT, that isn't who I am': An exploration of the experiences of career changer primary teachers in their first year of teaching. *Teachers and Teaching: Theory and Practice, 16*(4), 461-475.

Piaget, J. (1952). *The origins of intelligence in children.* Norton.

Richardson, L. (1994). Writing: A method of inquiry. In N. Denzin & Y. Lincoln (Eds.), *Handbook of qualitative research* (pp. 516-529). Sage.

Saldaña, J. (2011). *Fundamentals of qualitative research.* Oxford University Press.

Shields, C. M. (2010). Transformative leadership: Working for equity in diverse contexts. *Educational Administration Quarterly, 46*(4), 558-589.

St. Pierre, Elizabeth Adams. (2011). Post-qualitatitive research: The critique and the coming after. In N. K. Denzin & Y. S. Lincoln (Eds.), *The Sage handbook of qualitative research* (4th ed., pp. 611-625). Sage.

St. Pierre, E. (2000). Poststructural feminism in education: An overview. *Qualitative Studies in Education, 13*(5), 477-515.

Starkey, L. (2010). Supporting the digitally able beginning teacher. *Teaching and Teacher Education, 26*(7), 1429-1438.

Strom, K. J. (2014). *Becoming-teacher: The negotiation of teaching practice of first- year secondary science teachers prepared in a hybrid urban teacher education program* (Doctoral Dissertation, Montclair State University).

Strom, K. J. (2015). Teaching as assemblage: Negotiating learning and practice in the first year of teaching. *Journal of Teacher Education, 66(*4), 321-333.

Strom, K., Margolis, J., & Polat, N. (2019). Teacher professional dispositions: Much assemblage required. *Teachers College Record,* 121(11).

Strom, K., & Martin, A. (2017). *Becoming-teacher: A rhizomatic look at first-year teaching.* Sense.

Strom, K. & Martin, A. (2022). Toward a critical posthuman understanding of teacher development. *Teaching and Teacher Education.* Retrieved on 6/14/2024 from https://www.sciencedirect.com/science/article/pii/S0742051X22000592.

van Alfen, C. (1993, March). *School board policy as an instrument of empowering leadership in America.* Paper presented at the annual conference on Creating Quality Schools, Oklahoma City, OK.

Veenman, S. (1984). Perceived problems of beginning teachers. *Review of Educational Research, 54*(2), 143-178.

Villegas, A. M. (2007). Dispositions in teacher education: A look at social justice. *Journal of Teacher Education,* 58(5), 370-380.

Vygotsky, L. S. (1978). *Mind in society: The development of higher psychological processes.* Harvard University Press.

Waldrop, M. M. (1993). *Complexity: The emerging science at the edge of order and chaos.* Simon and Schuster.

Zeichner, K. (2010). Rethinking the connections between campus courses and field experiences in college- and university-based teacher education. *Journal of Teacher Education, 61*(2), 89-99.